Commentaries
on the
Book of Wisdom

Commentaries
on the
Book of Wisdom

Russell Marlett

ReadersMagnet, LLC

Commentaries on the Book of Wisdom
Copyright © 2022 by Russell Marlett

Published in the United States of America
ISBN Paperback: 978-1-957312-36-1
ISBN eBook: 978-1-957312-37-8

All rights reserved. No part of this publication may be reproduced, stored in a retrieval system or transmitted in any way by any means, electronic, mechanical, photocopy, recording or otherwise without the prior permission of the author except as provided by USA copyright law.

The opinions expressed by the author are not necessarily those of ReadersMagnet, LLC.

ReadersMagnet, LLC
10620 Treena Street, Suite 230 | San Diego, California, 92131 USA
1.619. 354. 2643 | www.readersmagnet.com

Book design copyright © 2022 by ReadersMagnet, LLC. All rights reserved.
Cover design by Ericka Obando
Interior design by Don Anderson

Contents

Summary vii
Chapter I 1
Chapter II 4
Chapter III 8
Chapter IV 10
Chapter V 14
Chapter VI 17
Chapter VII 20
Chapter VIII 26

THE BOOK OF WISDOM

One 27
Two 28
Three 29
Four 30
Five 31
Six 32
Seven 33
Eight 34
Nine 35
Ten 36
Eleven 37
Twelve 38

Thirteen 39
Fourteen 40
Fifteen 41
Sixteen 42
Seventeen 43
Eighteen 44
Nineteen 45
Twenty 46
Twenty-One 47
Twenty-Two 48
Twenty-Three 49
Twenty-Four 50
Twenty-Five 51
Twenty-Six 52
Twenty-Seven 53
Twenty-Eight 54
Twenty-Nine 55
Thirty 56
Thirty-One 57
Thirty-Two 58

Chapter IX 59
Chapter X 62
Epilogue 67

Summary

What would your reaction be if you were a ten year old who was shown a locked chest, but then forbidden to open it? Would you obediently walk away, and put it out of mind – eventually forgetting that you had ever seen it? Or, would the realization that the chest existed drive your imagination to the point of believing that the assumed value of the chest's contents would support a lavish lifestyle for a lifetime? Human nature being what it is, I think man of us would want to believe the latter.

Over time, an optimistic, hopeful ten year old grew into a disillusioned pessimist who blamed the world for his self inflicted, perceived failure. Hope was rekindled when a chest he had coveted from childhood came into his possession through an inheritance. Hope was dashed when his initial examination of the contents did not indicate that they were of any tangible value, whatsoever. The last item in the chest was a time worn and bound envelope that he opened more out of curiosity than anticipation, yet – when its contents were revealed they were found to be like gold of a different color and a higher value.

Chapter I

In the eyes of a ten-year-old boy there is always treasure inside a chest that can't be opened. That's a characteristic common to all treasure chests, really. As long as they remain locked, one can imagine their contents to be enough gold and jewels to buy an entire country, or to finance an expedition to one of the other planets in our solar system, or to pay a professional basketball player's salary for a year. The possibilities are limitless, but they are so only if the trunk remains unopened.

I was ten the first time I saw my own personal treasure chest. It was a great box with a rounded top whose stout oak sides, bound by massive iron straps, shouted, "Why would anyone build anything as strong as me if they didn't have something valuable to hide inside?" The chest was in Great Aunt Prudence's attic, where I was forbidden to be, unaccompanied by an adult, which is naturally the reason the attic held such a fascination for me.

There were a number of reasons that the chest had to contain a vast treasure. Number one, it was hidden bags in the corner of the attic. Numerous boxes had to be moved aside in order to find the chest, and the boxes were stacked so that --to this young sleuth--their sole purpose was to cover up what could only be a trove so vast that it would be a magnet for thieves if its presence were known. Number two, the very fact that the house that Great

Aunt Prudence lived in had been built by her grandfather who was a captain of a whaling ship and a seafaring man made it a certainty that the chest had been discovered by him in one of his journeys and brought to the house where it was put back in the corner of the attic and not discovered until I found it again, nearly a hundred years later. Number three, it was locked and try as I might, I could not get it to open. Reason number three was the clincher, and I knew that I had made the find of the century.

My find of the century was very paradoxical in that while I would undoubtedly become a celebrity when I announced it, the very fact that I had found it in a place where I was not supposed to be made the announcement an impossibility. In looking back, it's just as well that it happened that way because the knowledge of the chest sparked hope within me for the next quarter of a century--the last eight years of which I endured but didn't live because of a job I couldn't stand but was afraid to leave.

The summer of my great discovery was the only time I ever visited Great Aunt Prudence. She was my mama's aunt. We lived in Texas and Great Aunt Prudence lived in Massachusetts where Gra'ma had lived until she decided to move away from winter and teach school in warmer climes. When she got to Texas, she turned low born in a hurry and wound up married to an oil field roughneck with a reputation for fighting, drinking, and being a favorite of some of the more adventurous ladies of the East Texas oil patch. She straightened his ass out in a hurry, as one of their contemporaries explained when he was relating some of their early experiences at my granddaddy's funeral, and by the time I could remember anything Granddaddy was a pillar of the Methodist church in Beaumont.

Granddaddy and Gra'ma begot Mama, and stopped there, so our family wound up being Great Aunt Prudence's only living close kin. Gra'ma and Prudence did have a brother, Ezra Burton, but he had not been heard from in my mama's lifetime and the only thing she knew about him was that he went to sea before Gra'ma lit out for Texas. There was one old photograph of the three of them when they were children. Gra'ma and Ezra were smiling mischievously, but Great Aunt Prudence was scowling like she had bitten into something that had bitten back. That was the thing that perplexed me the most when I met her for the first time. She was so displeased with everything before it happened that nothing ever happened to please her, while Gra'ma was one of those people that could find something to laugh about in the aftermath of a hurricane. When we did go up to Massachusetts to visit Great Aunt Prudence, I had sort of hoped that she would be just like Gra'ma who laughed a lot and could think up all sorts of neat things to do with a kid my age. But she was not like Gra'ma. My first clue came during the first five minutes of our one and only vacation to Massachusetts. I called her Aunt Pru, when we were introduced, and she bored a hole through me with a stare of displeasure, then started in on an explanation of what a great aunt was, and ended up-almost an hour later-by saying I could call her Great Aunt Prudence. She sort of loosened up during the next two weeks, but not much.

 In retrospect, in her own way, she was the catalyst for change in my life. If she had not taken me up to the attic, ushered me through the door, let me see the collection from over a hundred years of occupation by the same family, then forbidden me to ever set foot up there-unaccompanied by an adult-I never would have discovered the chest and the unbelievable treasure that did lie inside.

Chapter II

Becoming a human adult is a perilous undertaking. What I mean by this is, well, think of a coyote. When a coyote is born, it is destined to eat rabbits and howl at the moon. Not so with a human child. Our destinies are in our own hands, which causes a lot of confusion and discomfort in many of us because it would be a lot more comfortable if we had it all laid out for us. It is my personal opinion that the desire for predictability leads to the demand for conformity in our social, commercial, educational and religious institutions and this implied demand causes us no end of agony when we are confronted by choice. I think about the choices I made that got me into the dead-end life I was living. It seems that my primary criterion for choosing one option over another was what was expected of me rather than what suited my desires and capabilities. It would have been simple to have been born a coyote, but it turned out to be so exciting to be human. At least it did, once I caught on to how to be human to the fullest extent of the concept.

When we got back home-which was Houston at the time-from Massachusetts, I went back to my comfortable routine of playing sports games and war games and board games with my buddies. I also went swimming and spent a lot of time scratching mosquito bites. When I became a teenager the battle with zits was added to the discomfort of mosquito bites, and we cut out playing the games for the sake of fun and began playing them for the sake of winning. It was society's and nature's way of preparing us for adulthood. We became more conscious of appearance than substance, and more aware of self-worth based on final scores of the various competitions we participated in than in self-worth based on accomplishment of personal goals. There were an awful lot of us who reached our majorities believing that we were ugly losers.

Somewhere along the line, in my upbringing, I was introduced to the "work ethic" which seemed to be that if one put in enough time at a task one would be compensated and could thus eke out a living without being a burden on society. Burdens on society were pointed out to me as anyone on welfare and who would not even try to look for work. I grew up with a work ethic that was adopted by so many of my contemporaries, and that was to look for the remuneration over what was required for remuneration. The few of my childhood acquaintances who chose to learn as much as they could about the things that they were interested in and then become successful through pursuit of a goal of becoming proficient in their field of interest were looked on as lucky rather than directed. By age thirty five my biography read: He finished high school, like he was supposed to; he went to college, like he was supposed to; he got a job, like he was supposed to; he got married, like he was supposed to; they had children, like they were supposed to. None of the above was a real accomplishment from the standpoint of being anything I had chosen and then struggled to accomplish. I finished high school because I kept going to school for twelve years. I got out of college with a degree in business, which was picked for me when I couldn't make up my mind about what I wanted to take. I took my first job because my father, who had taken over Granddaddy's hardware store, got me an interview with one of his suppliers and they told me they would hire me as a management trainee. I got married to the same girl I had gone with since eighth grade because neither one of us could bear the uncertainty of starting a relationship with someone else. The marriage was typical of a couple whose only attraction for one another was sex at a time in their lives when hormones were raging so rampantly in their bodies that anyone who would help relieve the pressure could become a love object. By the time we were in our early twenties, sex with each other was a convenience and-quite frankly-both of us were seeking other partners for excitement, even though it was something we didn't acknowledge. By some stroke of fortune, we held an unexciting marriage together, primarily because there were children involved, and did not succumb to the trap of "personal fulfillment" as a reason for going separate ways to cater to our own desires. When I look back on all that happened, staying together despite the boredom was probably one of the better things we ever did.

That's where I was in my life when the letter came that was the first step in a miraculous change. It was from a law firm in Massachusetts, and the gist of it was that since I was one of Great Aunt Prudence's only close kin still living, I was remembered in her will. I became very excited about the prospects of receiving a large check representing great wealth until I reread the letter. Great Aunt Prudence had never gotten on that well with people, so she gave all her money to various animal protection and benevolence organizations and left the people-namely me-the personal effects in her attic.

The letter had arrived on a Friday, and I was on a plane for Boston the next Thursday. Heidi didn't seem to care one way or another whether I went or stayed and had no desire to go up there with me. I guess her attitude about my trip should have been a clue that our marriage was on rockier ground than I realized. The kids kept pressing me for indications of what I was promising to bring back with me that they could break and discard within thirty minutes of taking it out of its box. When my east bound 727 left the ground that morning, a great weight seemed to fall from me, and I began to have thoughts about what it would be like not to have to go back. It wasn't the first time those thoughts had occurred.

Chapter III

It was shortly after midnight when the flight landed in Boston. I was tired. We'd had just enough unused credit on one card to cover the flight and a rental car, but not enough to squeeze in the luxury of a hotel. If we'd stopped to analyze it, maybe a lot of our discontent with our marriage came from the fact that our two modest incomes were used up by credit card and other indebtedness before they were earned. We were so far behind that if either one of us had lost a job, we'd be homeless. But we had a house full of electronic gimmickry, some of which still worked.

It doesn't take long to get anywhere in Massachusetts, at least when you compare it to going someplace in Texas. Despite getting lost twice and stopping for coffee, I reached my destination quicker than I intended to. It was still dark when I parked outside the immaculate two-story frame house surrounded by a white picket fence. Not even the neatly lettered sign imbedded in the manicured lawn, telling the observant passer-by that this was an attorney's office, could destroy the initial image of this being the home of somebody in a Norman Rockwell calendar painting.

I slept fitfully in the car until the town constable knocked on my window to ask if everything was okay. Dawn was breaking when he had awakened me and despite my best efforts, I couldn't get back to sleep. I stiffly pulled myself out of the car and moved slowly and gingerly to a bench at the corner of the block. My body had been in a seated position for most of the past ten hours, and my muscles weren't quite ready to stretch out and move. The walk to the bench, coupled with the lack of sleep, exhausted me. Just one more reminder that the exercise routine I kept intending to start was overdue.

Things started happening once I reached the bench and resumed the seated posture of the past half day. The first thing that happened was that I became aware of how fresh and clean the air was. The next thing that struck my senses was how quiet it was. In Houston, we lived two blocks from a freeway, and exhaust fumes and traffic roar were constant and inescapable parts of our home life. I sat on that bench for three hours, until the lawyer's office opened, and never once heard a siren. I wondered if the people who lived in the impeccably neat houses that I could see from the bench worried about things like burglaries, drive by shootings, getting robbed at gun point in the grocery store parking lot, things that were part of our lives for twenty four hours of every day back in Houston. I wondered if maybe Heidi and I could ever afford to live in a place like this where our kids might be able to go to a school and concentrate on learning rather than survival in the halls and on the playground. No way that that could ever happen. The marriage wouldn't stay together long enough.

Chapter IV

Great Aunt Prudence's lawyer was distantly affable--if you can get that picture. It wasn't like back home where an introduction involves a hearty handshake, a slap on the back, and the impression that you are meeting a new friend for life. It didn't take long for him to go through the part about this more than likely being a wasted trip since there wasn't anything of value in the attic, sign here, and anything you want to take has to be out of the house before next Wednesday. Since I had to be back at work on Monday morning, Wednesday didn't have a lot of significance.

The lawyer sent me on my way, after handing the house key to his secretary, who looked like a woman his wife had hired. She was instructed to lead me out to the house and unlock it for me. When we got there, she didn't give me a lot of time to look around downstairs but marched me straight to the attic and opened the door. Anything in the attic was mine to take or leave, but don't even think about taking anything downstairs since what had not already been removed was destined for auction with the proceeds going to worthy animals. Just in case I would have the temerity to venture into forbidden territory, I was reminded that a crew from the auction house would be arriving at any time and would more than likely report any transgressions on my part to the secretary who was stern without being severe-a characteristic that seemed to pass for friendliness in that part of the country.

Attics are not customarily well lighted spaces, and my late Great Aunt Prudence's attic was no exception. The solitary small window at the gable end of the attic was cleaner than it would have been if it had been my attic window, but not quite as invisible glass clear as all the other windows in the house. The light that filtered in through it reflected off the infinite universe of dust motes which rose, fell, and swirled in the shafts of illumination that penetrated the divided panes in the window. The light created a strange perception of place. Everything in front of the window was clearly visible, but just to the sides of the well-defined light beams a shadowy world of boxes could be seen.

I had seen the place a thousand times in my memory, but I was shocked at how small the space actually was. When I had first seen the attic, it had seemed immense with unlimited space to store all sorts of rare and valuable artifacts just waiting to be discovered by a discerning ten year old. Now, my imagination dulled by the necessity of having had to acquiesce to practicality and reality for more years than not, it became apparent that the only things up there were items discarded because they were no longer of any use or value to the occupant who had placed them there. A cursory examination of the contents of selected boxes was a commentary on the technology explosion of the mid to late twentieth century. The majority of the discards were no older than the nineteen fifties and were-in almost all cases-small household appliances or personal care items with electrical cords attached. In a house that old, I had hoped to find a number of antique odds and ends that would fetch exorbitant prices when brought out and sold.

Of course, what I really wanted to get into was the trunk. The reason I hadn't gone directly to it was because of the plan I had formulated on the plane coming to Boston. The reasoning went something like, if I open the trunk first, I will probably be so overwhelmed with the riches inside that I will quit searching the other boxes, and will therefore overlook a number of other things of great value. Wrong. The only thing consistent about the other boxes in the attic is that they all seemed to be filled with Goodwill discards.

It was soon time to open the trunk. It wasn't hard to find because it hadn't been moved from its spot of a quarter century before, I pulled it out into the open space in the midst of the boxes and stared at it. This thing was going to be a piece of cake because the hasp lock banged loosely against it when I moved it, which showed me that it wasn't even locked.

On second thought, that was a bad sign. I had distinctly remembered the chest being locked when I had first discovered it. Anger flooded into my consciousness. Some son of a bitch had beaten me to the treasure. The anger drained from me, seemingly taking everything else inside with it because I went into a kind of limp, empty, slack jawed trance of disappointment and damned near cried.

How could this happen? That treasure had been mine. It was the hope I had clung to over the years. When things weren't going the way I wanted them to, the thought of the treasure in the old chest had given me the hope that someday I would be rich enough to buy my own way and to hell with the rest of them. The thoughts were particularly strong in the days when Heidi selfishly jumped down my throat about playing golf on the weekends, after I had been on the road the previous five days, or spending Saturday and Sunday watching the games. She never seemed to consider the pressure I was under, and my need to get some relaxation. The kids were part of it, too. They would never cut me any slack. Always pestering me for something. The chest had been my escape route. My chest of hope, and now that hope had just flown out the window. It had to be empty. It hadn't even felt very heavy when! had dragged it out into the open.

I was beginning to become angry again, and the anger was building into rage, the rage of helpless and hopeless. I didn't even want to look inside, now. I kicked the chest and turned and stormed toward the attic door. There was a small cardboard box in my path, and I kicked it too. It flew up against a rafter, ricocheted back at me and the corner caught me just beneath my eye. I could feel blood trickling down my cheek when I reached the door, but I didn't care.

Downstairs, I began to relax, but I was still mad. At the front door, I looked out and I saw the truck of the crew from the auction house pulling up to the curb. I looked at my watch. It wasn't even ten o'clock yet, and I had until Sunday evening to hang around the area.

I had had to talk my way into this trip. Heidi hadn't wanted me to take it because we just couldn't afford to spend money on a wild goose chase. If I came back home empty handed, I would have to listen to it for at least a week. There was enough money in my pocket for meals and not much else. The only place I could go was back to the rent car, which was going to be my home until my return flight. The prospect of finding anything fun and affordable to kill time was bleak.

I felt the blood on my cheek. It was starting to congeal but had not yet turned crusty. What the hell, I told myself. Looking through those god dammed boxes will at least give me something to do. I climbed back into the attic and stood in front of the chest. Okay, sucker. I'll open you now.

Chapter V

The lid came up easily, and from the open chest there came an aroma of some kind of balsam like fragrance. In the top of the chest was a tray filled with a strange assortment of printed materials, letters, and odds and ends like a linen handkerchief, a silver spoon, a small china doll, and other items that to a casual observer might look like junk but they were packed away too carefully to be discards. One of the printed items was a dance card. I remembered Gra'ma telling me about dance cards. When she and Great Aunt Prudence were young, dances were called balls and all the girls were issued dance cards which they tied to their wrists. If a guy wanted to dance with a particular girl, he had to write his name on her card beside whatever dance number was open. The card in the chest was full of names, but William Morgan seemed to have signed up for most of the dances. He was also the one who had written almost all of the letters addressed to Miss Prudence Burton which were neatly tied together and tucked away squarely in the corner of the tray.

I wasn't that interested in finding out what had happened to William Morgan, but I did wonder if he and Great Aunt Prudence had ever got it on. Probably not. I stuck the silver spoon in my pocket and picked up the tray.

The next layer was comprised of correspondence that went back to eighteen ninety-seven. The oldest letter was addressed to Mrs. Sarah Burton and children and was from Captain Amos Burton. There was no return address, only the notation that he was on the SS Esther Morgan in Sidney, Australia. It made me wonder whether Ester was Williams's mother. If she was, and if the Morgan's were owners of the ship that my great grandfather captained, then maybe William had taken advantage of his position of power and of Great Aunt Prudence and had his way with her before casting her aside for another. The cad.

Judging from the number of letters in the chest, the family was comprised of prolific correspondents. The handwriting on the envelopes was almost artwork in the various whirls and sweeping lines that made the letters of the names and addresses on them. One of the more noticeable scripts was on an envelope from First Mate Ezra Burton on the SS Goodhue, and was sent from Colon, Panama. It was from Great Uncle Ezra. I was very curious to read something from him. Gra'ma had told me stories about the things she and her brother would get into, and how she missed him. He had gone to sea after she left for Texas, and she had not heard anything from him since.

Along with the personal correspondence were a few business papers, only one of which held any interest for me. It was a certificate for ten thousand shares of a company called The Great Columbia Gold Mine and was made out to Amos Burton as owner of record. I stuck that in my pocket in the hope that I could track it down to its modern-day identity and discover that I had indeed become a billionaire from Great Aunt Prudence's unintended generosity.

I was not as meticulous in emptying the trunk as Great Aunt Prudence had been in filling it, and the contents were scattered haphazardly around the floor by the time I got to the bottom.

The last item I came to was a large manila envelope, wrapped in twine with a note clipped to the top. Neither the note nor the envelope had a date showing.

By this time, I could tell who was who by the handwriting, and the envelope was from Ezra. The note had been written by Great Aunt Prudence. It certainly got my attention when I read it.

> To Whoever Finds This Packet:
>
> The contents of this attached envelope must be destroyed. I cannot bring myself to do it because this may be the last correspondence I will have from my dear, misguided brother. His soul has obviously been captured by Satan because only the Devil could force him to write the things he has written. I cannot bear to reveal what he has sent me to anyone, so mine will be the only prayers to our Lord and Savior asking for Brother's forgiveness. I hope that a gracious and loving God will hear them, and that our family will be united in a Heavenly Paradise when we have all answered the last roll call. The thought of poor Ezra writhing in the agony of eternal fire is more than I can stand.
>
> Prudence Burton

There were three reasons for opening the big envelope. I had a lot of time left, it was the last envelope in the chest, and who could resist reading a message from the Devil himself?

Chapter VI

One of the character traits instilled in me by Granddaddy was to have a good pocketknife I my person at all times. On the day I found the envelope, I was particularly glad that I had developed this habit. I don't know what the string was made of that bound Ezra's envelope, but it was still sturdy after all the years it had been at the bottom of the trunk. Also, Great Aunt Prudence knew her knots, because the string was taut, and the knots were like iron and couldn't be budged. My knife made short work of them, and I opened the envelope. Inside was what appeared to be a long letter from Ezra. It was written on a material that had the appearance and feel of heavy vellum but was-in some undefinable way-different.

The letter was undated, and all that was noted before the Dearest Sister Prudence part was the name Guatemala. I didn't have to read much of it to know that I would have liked my great uncle. He had been an adventurer.

> Dearest Sister Prudence,
>
> I hope this correspondence finds you well and in good spirits. Give my regards to our beloved sister, Esther and to Mama and Papa if they are still among the living. I have been out of touch for so long that I am sure you have

been in great doubt as to my continued presence here on Earth. I assure you that I am in fine fettle, and-but for a bullet which I somehow acquired in Port Said-have no complaints. The afore mentioned bullet was a gift from a port official who had no capacity for alcohol, and it makes its presence known quite frequently when a weather change is imminent.

Guatemala is a beautiful country, albeit one in which too many of the inhabitants are relegated to lives of grinding poverty. I got here after our ship struck a hazard, off the coast of Panama, and sank almost immediately. Several of my shipmates were lost at sea, but eight of us survived. We were three days in a lifeboat before finding land, and I can assure you that the constant exposure to the tropical sun did neither my constitution nor my disposition any benefit.

When we felt fully recovered from our ordeal, Ned Carter, the third officer and I decided to try our hands at gold prospecting rather than sign on another vessel. We settled on Guatemala as a destination and made the trip overland. What a trip it was. Three months on mule trails and cart paths through dense jungles full of poisonous vipers and other deadly fauna not the least of which is the jaguar. The worst beasts of the lot were the officials who are nothing but brigands with badges, and who are more treacherous than the vipers.

Several months after reaching Guatemala, it became apparent that our gold mining venture was destined to be as unsuccessful as Papa's so Ned took off overland for a port on the east coast and I decided to explore some of the ancient mounds that the natives had led me to in the jungle. Initially my motives for wanting to explore these mounds were very base. I became a grave robber in the hope of discovering treasures. Ironically, my search for treasures of gold brought me to this place where I found the greatest treasure of all. It is this I wish to share with you, and tender into your care for safekeeping.

Before I tell you the story of this treasure, I must divulge that I have always detested the pompous piety that our religious institutions practice under the guise of worship of some contradictory god. Yet, under the canopy of stars at night the predictable order of their positions in the various seasons is reason enough for me to believe that there is a power that has brought all this into being, and rules it still. It is nigh on to impossible for me to equate this power with the god of Reverend Allison who will punish us for the frailties of the body that he created for us by throwing our souls into a fiery hell for an eternity. On the other hand, we are promised that if we completely ignore the urges that the flesh of this God created body impose upon our beings we will be rewarded by an eternity in a heaven that is very bland, and devoid of joy. In all honesty, I would be hard put to choose between an eternity in Reverend Allison's heaven, and one merry night of revelry with my mates. Having said this, I can now continue with the story of the newfound treasure.

This was the end of the letter portion of Ezra's papers. The next page was formatted differently, almost like a book. I thumbed the pages of what was left to read and wondered if I really wanted to take the time to finish. The light in the attic was fading, and through the attic window I could see overcast skies that gave a promise of rain. Below, I could hear the crew from the auction house sorting and carting out what was left of the furnishings. The attic was comfortable, I was comfortable, so what the heck. Besides, there was not a little curiosity about what this treasure was that he mentioned. I decided to read on.

Chapter VII

A moonless night in a jungle is a night like I have never experienced in any other environment. The oppressive, wet stillness of the air allies itself with the rife, surrounding vegetation to build a thick cloud cover that blots out even the brightest light from the canopy of distant stars. The blackness inside my hut seemed to devour the light from a flickering oil lamp I was reading by, and the circle of light cast by the lamp did not even encompass all of the crude table that it sat upon.

I had just closed the covers on the well-thumbed pages of a book of essays by Emerson and was rubbing my tired eyes when I felt another presence in the room. I struggled to stifle any signs of the fear rising up within me. I was a hundred miles from a society bound by law - a thousand miles from one that provided a modicum of justice. An intruder here, and at this time of night could surely only mean that my possessions were at risk, and that quite possibly my life was also.

The pistol which has been my constant companion lo these many years was lying beneath the pillow of my cot which itself was surrounded by mosquito netting neatly tucked under a thin mattress. I slowly lowered my hands and placed them in my lap in plain view of the imagined intruder. I peered into the darkness in the direction of the doorway. There was nothing to be seen, yet I knew someone was there.

My impulse was to rise from the chair and rush to the cot, where childlike - I would pull the covers over my head and wait out the night until the light of morning dispelled the demon, or whatever I felt was in my presence. As I sat and pondered plans of action, my visitor appeared-not all at once-but like a mist that swirls and eddies and forms itself into a being that becomes flesh and blood. By the time the whoever was standing firmly on the earthen floor before me, just enough into the circle of light to be perceived as a presence but not clearly lighted enough to be discerned in detail, my heart was pounding so hard that I feared it was trying to exit my body and escape the hut through a rear window. Any illusion that I might conceivably be in control of the situation was, I am sure, shattered when I weakly stammered out a request for the presence to identify itself.

What stood, before me was a person of modest height, clad in a one piece robe with a cowl that cast an impenetrable shadow over his face. He stood in silence for an interminable period of time before he spoke.

"I am The One Who Is. Before time was, I was. When time is ended, I will still be. Mankind has known me in the past. I am in the present. Mankind will see me in the future."

"What do you want here?" I stammered.

"You have been chosen," he replied.

"Chosen? For what?" I boldly asked. My fear was rapidly abating by now, and I was calculating whether or not to rush my uninvited guest and wrestle him out the door. I was obviously larger than he was and quite probably stronger, but I still wasn't sure whether or not he was armed.

"To receive the truth." He reached inside a sleeve of his garment and pulled out a sheaf of paper which he handed to me. "When I tell you, you will write."

This, of course, is the paper he handed me. It is like no other I have seen in any port of the known world. I accepted it mutely and held it for several moments before asking my next question.

"Why? " was my dumbfounded response.

The figure in the robe seated himself across from me at the small table at which I took my meals, and on which I did my occasional correspondence. The table was bare except for the inadequate oil lamp and my books, ink pot and pen. Strangely, the light from the little oil lamp now filled the room, but the face of the stranger was still hidden in the shadow of the cowl.

Since the day I left the security of the home of my father I have always been accompanied by my pistol and my knife. These are my companions in the world of men. There have been a few times when these companions have preserved my life. When I can find sanctuary, then they are relegated to a corner, and the volumes in my small library become my friends. A small book of the writings of Lao Tse, one of Plato, Mr. Emerson's essays, and of course, the Bible which I grew up with but which I also question in part. It was to these that the interloper pointed as he spoke.

"You seek truth."

"Yes."

"I will tell you the truth. What you are about to be told is the Book of Wisdom. It existed at the beginning, it exists now, it will exist when time is no more. What it is now is not all that it is to be."

Those who know me well know that I am not an impatient man, and that I generally have time to hear even the most irrational of beings out. This being, however, was not easily categorized as either rational or irrational. Just the manner in which he had materialized before me gave him a modicum of credence as a bearer of some news or lore that I might be interested in at least hearing if not heeding, yet the things he was saying made me question his sanity. In all the ports of the world, in countries known and in those you have not even heard of, are the men who profess knowledge of greater destiny. In rags or in robes, they ply the streets and alley ways, buttonholing the unwary traveler and promising him heaven if he contributes to their cup or hell if he doesn't. I suppose you could say they are like the Reverend Allison, except that he does it inside a quite substantial building rather than in the streets. I began to wonder if my visitor had a cup of his own hidden up a sleeve of his garment.

"When the book was committed to the written word is not known. When it began, it was carried in the hearts of those to whom it was entrusted. As those to whom it is entrusted come to know it, they add to it as they are told to add to it."

"So, why don't you just write it down yourself and give it to me? It seems to me that if it is written already then to write it again is a waste of effort."

"Why I do what I do is not for you to know, but I will do this. If you can answer the three questions I will ask, then I will give you the book already written. Can we make a bargain? "

At the time, my only thought was, "What kind of fool do you take me for?" That was not my response, however.

"I think not." I replied. "There are things of science I have no knowledge of, as well as things of other lands and other languages. The things I know nothing of will fill more volumes than the things I know. How can I agree to answer three questions if I do not first know the subject they will pertain to?"

He was silent for a moment, and there was about his being a difference. I thought I could feel him smile, even though the lips that would show this action were invisible to me. "You do have the potential for wisdom. I know now why you were chosen."

My visitor rose from his chair and faced the books I had on my table. His hand swept the air before them. "Do you know these books?" he asked.

"They are all I have had to read for the time I have been here."

"If you have understood what they contain, then you will have no trouble answering my questions. Do we have a bargain?"

"How long is the thing you want me to write?"

"What you will write is truth. Truth needs few words for its telling."

"But if I answer your questions then you will give it to me already written. Is that correct?"

"That will be our bargain."

"And the questions cover a subject I should know?"

"You try my patience," he answered, but in a calm, almost hushed voice. "I will never trick you, nor deceive you. Now, agree that we have a bargain and we can get on with the business at hand."

The visitor who had initially aroused a sense of danger within me, had-in the time he had been in my presence-altered my feelings to the point that I had become very curious about what he could possibly say. After all, I reasoned, I could always just refuse to write if what he wanted me to take down was turning out to be a waste of my time.

"We have a bargain," I told him. "Please ask your questions."

"Very well," he responded quietly. He paused, then in a somewhat firmer voice asked, "What is God?" Another pause, "Who is God's prophet?"

He arose and stepped to the window. As he faced the blackness of the jungle nigh, I could see his hands clasped behind his back.

He was silent for almost a minute before he turned to face me again. "What is the purpose of mankind?" Came his final question.

Silence settled like a mantle on the room, and its weight seemed to descend upon me like that of a huge, heavy blanket. The cogs and levers of whatever machinery it is that fills my head whirred and clanked at a rate never before experienced. I opened my mouth to speak several times but realized that whatever I would say would be subjective and open to debate.

These strange questions that I had asked myself from time to time and had even answered on different occasions with-I must confess- different answers each time, were going to turn me into an amanuensis for the evening. I sat silent and dumbfounded, staring mutely at the tabletop before me.

"Can you answer the questions?" he finally asked. 'I'm not sure; I answered.

"Then fulfill our bargain and write what I tell you, and I will answer the questions."

My feelings about taking commands from this stranger are hard to describe. At the time I felt irritation at his effrontery, but there was a quality about him that piqued my curiosity and I was a bit anxious to know what he was going to say. I dipped my pen into the inkwell and waited for him to speak.

Chapter VIII

The Book of Wisdom

ONE

Before there was time, there was nothing
Then there was movement, and from movement came all things
All that is, is of the source
The source has no name
That which has a name is not the source
The source is the way to God, it exists only to serve
One who knows the source is a prophet
One who knows nothing is God.

I will tell you what this means. There is a power that has always been. It is beyond the ability of man to know. From itself it created all that is. We are what the power is, yet we cannot be the power. Men have felt the power or in brief glimpses witnessed it, yet it is too great to be known. Because they have known it to be, they have tried to name it and harness it with laws. The only thing that has come from the naming of God is bloodshed. What God is, is too vast to have a name, yet each name is fought over as though the name itself is the power that it tries to define. These things I am about to tell you will show you the way to the power that is the giver of all that is and is all that is. These things I am about to tell you will empower you to live more richly. These things I am about to tell you will empower you to conquer your fears, your pain, and your loneliness. These things I am about to tell you have been told before and will be told again, but will mankind ever learn them? This is The Book of Wisdom. What is within the pages I give you is not all that is, and all of the book is not yet written.

TWO

The source is the gift of God.
Within it is the power to do all things
What the pure heart asks will be given
What the pure heart seeks will be found
Man cannot say how things will come to be
The source brings all things according to its own laws
The source cannot violate its laws
All the laws of the source are not known by man

Because the power which made all is what we are, then nothing can be denied us. Our only limitation is our lack of understanding of what we are and what we can be. When we seek to be the power, we will fail. When we let the power become us, we will succeed. Because of our lack of understanding and knowing we call the ordinary miraculous.

THREE

The source is a mystery that cannot be known
What is known is not all that is
Who would tell of it would deceive
Who would tell of it would seek power
Power is sought by priests and kings.
Peace is sought by man
Peace comes when each is a priest and a king
Priests and kings must surrender all and serve others

Man is finite. The power from which he is created is infinite. Man cannot know the infinite, yet man can know of it. What man knows he learns. What he knows he cannot teach. When we are taught, we are under the power of the teacher. What the teacher tells us may not be understood as it is intended. The only teaching that can reveal truth is example, not words. What God has given is the power of speech. What man has invented is the art of language. What is of God is perfect. What is of man is imperfect. How can man teach perfection when the tool with which he teaches is imperfect? Perfection must be experienced to be known; it cannot be told. When you have put self aside to serve the need of another you have approached perfection.

FOUR

The source is a city with many gates
Enter your gate at peace with all others
Peace is freedom – freedom truth
Truth is the path to wisdom
Know that you do not know and be wise
Great truth needs few words for its telling
One who knows the source does not tell of it
One who tells of the source does not know it

Because what is infinite cannot be known, all that we understand of it is not all that is. What we know is what we have learned. What another knows is what another has learned. As we do not know another's heart, so also is our heart not known by others. What we see as true may not be true in their eyes. Therefore, do not waste your time condemning what another believes, but work to strengthen your own faith. Let the actions of your faith be a guide to one who is without faith. What is to be known is greater than what can be known. How can we tell of something we cannot know? How can we judge another's belief when we cannot know all that is to be known about our own?

FIVE

The source lies within
It is a gift already possessed
All that is good is of the source
All that is good is light
Into the eye that seeks the source comes only light
To see darkness is to await disaster
Rejoice in your laughter, your day of joy is here
Rejoice in your sorrow, your day of joy is yet to be

Things of the world come to try us. Things of the world cannot defeat us if we face them through the power that created us from itself, and which resides within us. The power within is only good. The world without is sometimes perceived as dark and evil. To use the power that is yours, always seek the good. To find the good in what is seen as evil is to have the power to overcome evil. Those who look only at the good will have light for their paths. Those who dwell on the evil that befalls them and do not seek to find a blessing within it will stumble in the darkness. Those who anticipate evil will know it. We are not promised freedom from wrong but are promised the power to do right. Only when we see the good in all that befalls us can we begin to know the power that will lead us to that which is right.

SIX

Life is a river that flows from the source to the source
The river sustains itself and all that it carries
Within the source there is enough and to spare
There is no want
To want is to be without, to know is to have
What you would have, know that you have
What you would be, be
To have all you must lose all

We are born into a world that provides for us all we need. Only our lack of faith denies us the good that is ours. All around us is abundance, but it is not realized if we see only what we lack. If a man is hungry, let him not want for food but let him give thanks for warmth and shelter. To say, "I'm hungry;" is to recognize a lack. To say, "I am grateful for warmth," is to recognize good fortune. Good fortune recognized will build upon itself until there is only good. Lack recognized will build upon itself until even what one had in the beginning will be lost.

In your gratitude, first recognize the power that made you then know that what you need is provided. What is provided is not given but is for the taking. Only when you can give without fear of being without can you possess the abundance that is yours.

SEVEN

The source knows no time but eternity
Eternity is unbounded and infinite
Man has no time but the moment
The past is a lesson learned, the future is yet to be
This moment is all we can know
The moment filled remains forever, the moment lost cannot be recalled
Regret not loss, each new moment is a new beginning
Within eternity are our moments, within a moment is eternity

God knows only sequence. Only man knows time. The only time that can be used is the moment before us. We cannot change the past. We cannot know the future. To waste the moment in regret of things past or anxiety over things yet to come is to lose the only time we have to use. What is lost cannot be recalled, yet a moment lost is followed by a moment new and unused. Wisely use each moment given you and walk forward through time to fulfillment. Lose the moment and dwell on its loss, and time marches past while you, mired in confusion and indecision, watch the happy parade as a lonely bystander instead of taking your place in its rollicking midst.

EIGHT

Life is all that exists
That which we call death is smoke
Life is the whole, death but a part
Life is a new road that never ends
All we can know of the road is at our feet
Death is a valley through which the road passes
The road to the mountain begins in the valley
Welcome death in its time because it leads us to the mountain top

Only those who fear death are those who have not sought the life that is real. The stem produces a bud that becomes a flower, and the flower dies when it turns to seed. We admire the beauty of the flower but overlook its purpose which is the seed. So, it is with this world. We are blinded to its purpose by our search for beauty that our senses can perceive. If all we see with are our senses, then we will fear the inevitable which is transition to a world that cannot be perceived by the senses of flesh and blood. What can be seen is not what is real. What is real cannot be seen. What we see as life is only a part of the road on which we travel through time. Let the time of death be selected for us. There are lessons to be learned that we might miss if we choose the time for ourselves. Lessons that might free us in times ahead to reach a destination that we cannot now know.

NINE

To live is to know heartbreak, love, sorrow, happiness, defeat and victory
Remember the love, remember the happiness
Dwell on the victory, put defeat behind
The things of life will come
You cannot hide from them
Death comes before its time to one who fears life
Who fears the things of life will know defeat
Who lives life by the Source knows victory

There are things of this life that belong to it alone. The struggles of the body in this world have their impacts on our soul. Our soul will carry us into the world that is yet to be. Prepare your soul for victory by recognizing only victory. Prepare your soul for joy by remembering only happiness. In this life are lessons that prepare us for what is to come. Learn to rejoice in victory with the enemy who thinks he has defeated you. Learn to love the one who has broken your heart. Learn that what saddens you may be the thing that gladdens another and rejoice in the gladness. To feel the sadness, to know the heartbreak, to be disheartened by defeat cannot be avoided. What cannot be avoided does not have to be forever. To dwell on misfortune leads us to expect misfortune. To dwell on good leads us to expect good things to come. To expect misfortune is to know fear. A life lived in fear is no life at all.

TEN

The road ahead is built on stones of the past
A builder selects only the good stone
All others are cast away
So must it be with you
Within the past there is much to choose
Times of strength, joy and victory are stones for your road
Defeat, disappointment and sorrow are worthless pebbles to be cast away
Build your road on the good stone and you will find the source

How can we expect good if we see only evil? Our expectations guide us to our destinations. The lessons we learn teach us what to expect. In the battle won, learn that you can win. In the battle lost dwell on how well you fought. Put out of your mind the disappointment of dreams not realized, and instead remember those times when your dreams were fulfilled. A moment of joy remembered can overcome the wounds of a year of sorrow. Put the sorrow away and dwell on the time of happiness. Who can put sorrow in its place and remember the good times will have good times to look forward to. Who dwells on the sorrow will not see the good when it comes. Who dwells on defeat will not know the victory when it is won. The things we choose to know from our pasts will be the things we experience in the times to come. One who chooses only the good knows that the pain of defeat will be soothed by the balm of a victory yet to be won; that today's tears will not last and that they will soon give way to laughter; and that the gloom of today's disappointment will be dispelled by the sunshine of tomorrow's joy.

ELEVEN

That which is true is of the source
As the source is true so must you be also
An untruth to one is an untruth to all
Who breaks a vow to one will break a vow to all
Who will not be true to others will not be true to self
Who will not be true to self cannot find the source
To always speak truth is to know peace
To always speak truth is to be one with the source

What we would have, we must be. The greatest gift is the gift of peace. To receive peace, we must live in peace. A life of deceit is one that can never know peace. An untruth spoken to deceive another or to gain an advantage plants a seed that will erupt into a vine that chokes life out of the deceiver. What turmoil we deliver to ourselves from the fear of being found out. Mistrust of all others is the result of our deception of even one who would believe us, and if we cannot trust others who can we turn to in our need? What we are cannot be changed by false words, but what we are is revealed by false words. These things are untruths that should not be spoken: To say that you will do something you do not intend to do. To say that you have something that you do not have. To say something that is wrong to convince another of your sincerity. To say something that is wrong to entice a someone to do your bidding. To say something that is wrong to discredit someone in the eyes of another. Only when you are true to others can you find truth for yourself.

TWELVE

Knowledge is of man, wisdom is of the source
Know the world and perish
Seek wisdom and live
What one chooses to know defines character
Character cannot be concealed by words
Character is not revealed by words
Deeds reveal one's character
Show good character and reveal the source

Knowledge is gained through learning. Wisdom is shown by our use of knowledge. It is easy to know the things of the world around us because these are the things that respond to the senses. What we think we know, we often know because it fulfills the desires of the senses not the emptiness of the soul. Only wisdom, the awareness of the power that made us and how we are served by it, can fill the emptiness of our soul. Knowledge can be taught. Wisdom can only be learned. There is much of the world to be known. Know what is good and right and it leads to wisdom. Knowledge can be told. Wisdom can only be shown. To show wisdom is to have character. One who has character does what is right and good and does not ask a reward. When we speak of our good deeds, we do not reveal good character. Neither can we hide our evil with talk of good deeds. Our character shows others how we believe in the one who has made us, and who gives to us all that is good in unlimited abundance. Gain wisdom and have good character. Good character honors the power that is all.

THIRTEEN

Because of unbelief man lives by law
Law is right that protects the weak
Law is wrong that exalts the king
Within the Source all are the same
So, must it be with the laws of man
Who makes the law is bound by the law just law exacts only its
   due, nothing more
Life is not man's law to take

The laws of God are the standards for good character. The laws of man are a compendium of what we fear in ourselves. One who makes the law seeks power over others because he sees himself as weak, yet mankind must have its laws until the day that all men live to obey the laws of the power which is all. Therefore, make laws which protect and not laws which punish. Let the lawgiver be under the same law as the lawbreaker, and do not let one be given more privilege than the other in court. Only the law that applies equally to all can be considered just. How can the rights of others be respected by those who are not equals under man's law. Only when law is just, only when law is to protect and not punish, only when law applies equally to all will it be obeyed. Only when man lives under the laws of the Creator will man live in peace.

FOURTEEN

As the Source does not judge, neither are you to judge
As you think, so will you be
Think no ill of others
You do not know another's heart
Do not condemn what you cannot understand
Know your own heart and make it pure
Know the source and be a light that guides
The light that guides has no time to condemn

Our self is who we see when we look into the face of another. What we know of ourselves is what we will expect of others. When we say that another has done wrong, could it be a wrong that we too are guilty of? Believe in the goodness of the one who made you, and who is in you and do only those things that reveal that goodness to others. Only those who strive to make themselves pure and who forgive the impure acts of others can know the goodness that is theirs. How can one who will not forgive expect to be forgiven? How can one who would judge escape judgment? See yourself as good and expect that good to be in others. Until you know all that is in another's heart, you cannot know another's motives. Is it possible for evil acts to come from pure intentions? One who is good can see all others as good. One who is good is like a light in the darkness that others can see and follow. Light does not struggle with the darkness to be seen. Light is, and where there is light, there can be no darkness. To condemn another is to struggle with darkness. Therefore, make yourself good so that others can see the light of your goodness and be guided by it.

FIFTEEN

All that is love is of the source
Love fulfils needs, not desires
Love can only be given
Love is
Love in action cannot be defeated
Love in inaction cannot be overcome
Armed with love one cannot be destroyed
Know the source and be love

What love is we already possess. To say that we have been loved when our desires have been fulfilled is to say we have taken from another. Love is what we give of what we already have in abundance. When what we give must be given back, then we have not loved. Love is a sharing that dispels loneliness overcomes fear, and erases sorrow. The gift of love does not make the recipient dependent on the giver. The gift of love is not a gift of pleasure. The pleasure of love between man and woman is a sharing of trust. One who can love is never alone, is never fearful and is not burdened with sorrow. One who can love experiences the victory that awaits all who discover the reality of life.

SIXTEEN

Do to others only those things you want done to you
Protect the weak
Do only good, give only Love
The greatest will master self
The Least will master others
To master self and serve others is to be one with the source
See the source with your thoughts
Reveal the source with your deeds

Give to your neighbor only what you would wish to receive. To cause strife for another does not bring peace to you. What we give we also receive. Give strife and live in strife. Give peace and live in peace. Put out of mind the things you count as wrongs from another and give only as you would want to receive. Lend your strength to victims of poverty and ignorance. Return good when evil has been handed yow Give love in exchange for abuse and hatred. An enemy that is strong in combat is crushed beyond mending when confronted with love from the one he would destroy. Love does not control another. To share the love that is yours, serve others needs and not their demands. Deep within lies your source of love. Find your love in times of quiet. Show the love that is from the source of all love by your actions.

SEVENTEEN

The path to wealth does hot lead to the source
The path to the source does not lead to want
The heart that seeks wealth will never be filled
The heart that seeks the source will never know want
To know want is to know fear
To know the source is to have faith
Where faith lives, fear cannot abide
Where faith lives, there also abides the source

Things unseen are the greatest. Things of this world are the least. What is seen, felt, and coveted is too often what we strive to attain. Because we have to reach within ourselves to find them, the things that are real are too often overlooked. What is counted as wealth does not last past the grave, yet what is unseen is eternal. What is unseen nurtures and protects and cannot be taken away. What is grasped as wealth is coveted by others and can be lost more easily than it can be gained. Fear of loss keeps us from sharing the abundance of life with those whom it would benefit. To be truly wealthy, use wisely what is given you and share your wealth with others. To know that you will never be without is to live without fear.

EIGHTEEN

Good is of the source, greed is of man
The source leads, man acts
Actions guided by the source produce good
Actions guided by greed produce strife
Greed is born of desire
Want not what belongs to your neighbor
What you covet cannot be possessed
Share what is yours and do not take what is another's

What we believe ourselves to be is what we will give to others. If we believe deep within of our goodness, then good is what we will pass on to others in all that we do. Within each of us is the power that is all good, and each of us has the ability to take our Earth taught selves out of the way and let that power be us. Think only of the good you can do for your neighbor and give only good things-free of desire for good in return-and you will have revealed the Creator that is the source of all good. Gather the things of the world to you and keep them from being a benefit to your neighbor in need, and you have blocked the light that can shine from within you. To desire the things your neighbor has only causes strife. If you take them you will have made an enemy, and what is desirable to you will also be desirable to one more powerful than you. We are here for only a short time, and the things that are for this time will be left behind when we are no longer here. Share what is of this world with those who have not experienced your good fortune and you will have a treasure never ceasing.

NINETEEN

One who trades provides for one who plants
One who plants feeds one who weaves
One who weaves clothes one who trades
One cannot be without the others
Therefore, one is not greater, but all are the same
Where one is great another will be least
To the source there are no great or least
See all others as your equals and know the source

When one is exalted another is insignificant. This is the way of man. The way of man is the way of strife. Mankind is one with all that is, and one with the power of creation. When each one is lauded for each one's contribution to the whole then there is contentment and peace. Some must lead while others must follow yet without followers there cannot be a leader. Therefore, those who lead must serve those who follow as those who follow serve the leaders. What one produces in the way of goods is not more vital than what another produces in the way of goods. The jewelry of the goldsmith adorns the body of the king and is admired by all. The food from the farmer fills the body of the king yet is unseen after it is eaten. Whose contribution is most important? Whose is the least? Who has the wisdom to say? Because we cannot say which is the greatest, then we cannot honor one over others. All who contribute to the good of others are equals. Recognize the equality of all and do not strive to be acclaimed as greater than another. Only when you know the equality of all can you also know of the power that is all.

TWENTY

The gifts of the source come through the hands of man
The source gives the clay
Hands make the pot
There is no meat for one who will not hunt
There is no bread for one who will not plant
There is no shelter for one who will not build
Live in abundance through the work of your hands
Share your abundance and watch it grow

In the eyes of the power which made us there is no separation. Man is one with the power, one with himself, and one with the earth he inhabits. All that is needed to sustain life, and to let us prosper, is here for us. What is given must be used as it is given. Is the tree given you as houses already built? Is the ox given you as roasted meat? Is wool on the sheep's back as finished cloth? No. Man has taught himself to use these gifts for his greater good. Only the ones who will seek to fashion into the things of man, from what is given by the Source of all that is, will live in abundance. And do not be misled into believing the only gifts to man are gifts seen. What is put here for mankind to use is the seen and the unseen. Who can see knowledge? Who can see wisdom? Use what is given in the way that you can for the benefit of all. Teach others to do the same. Share what is given for all with those who are not yet able to see the gifts that are theirs. When all share, all live in plenty.

TWENTY-ONE

Out of the source come many yet all are one
Who has strength serves one with skill
Who has skill serves one with strength
The warrior protects the poet
The poet amuses the warrior
None are greatest, none are least
To each is given a talent
Find your talent and live in harmony with the one

In the eyes of the Creator all mankind is one. In the eyes of man, we are separate. The Creator has made us to serve the whole as we have been given the power to serve. The Creator does not know one task to be more important than another. Only man accords degrees of worth to things that must be done so that all may prosper. A king without a horse cannot be great in battle, yet the one who tends the horse is looked on as being lowlier than the king. One cannot be without the other. Serve as you are given the ability to serve and honor others for the service they render according to their abilities. Do not envy others for the talents they display or the roles they fill. Do not accord yourself honor for a talent you see as superior to another's. Choose to do what you have the ability to do, and do not ask for more. Abundance and happiness are the lot of those who are content and competent in the duties they perform.

TWENTY-TWO

Pick the ripe fruit from your tree
A man with no legs should not enter a foot race
Yet a slow runner may become fast with practice
The source gives to each a talent
Use the talent that is yours to provide for yourself
Use the talent that is yours to serve others
Give thanks to the source for the talent that is yours
Envy of another's talent does not honor the source

No one will be born into the Creator's world who cannot be used for the Creator's greater good. Each one is born with an ability or abilities that are discovered in the journey through this world. Some are born with more than others. This is the way of life. Those who see their abilities as less must not envy those who seem to have more. Those with more must not exalt themselves over those who seem to have less. All serve as they are given to serve. To do otherwise is to dishonor the Creator. The more we use the talent we discover in ourselves the greater things we can accomplish with it. To neglect our own talent because of envy of another's is to dishonor the Creator whose gift our talent is. We are provided for through the talents given us by our Creator. We serve others with our talents without asking to be served in return. When all serve, all are provided for, and the world is as it is intended to be.

TWENTY-THREE

The source gives equally to all
The source gives abundance, men seek wealth
Where there is wealth, there is poverty
Who has wealth must serve the one without wealth
Poverty is served by knowledge
Teach the hungry to plant and reap
Teach the naked to weave
One is enriched by what is shared, not what is hoarded

Why should there be want in the midst of plenty? It is because the eyes of men see only what is made by the hands of men as desirable. When wealth is measured by the goods of this world then those who do not possess these goods are called poor. When people are called poor, they come to believe themselves to be poor. There should be no poor. There should be no rich. To say there should be no rich does not say that there should be no possessions. They have possessions who believe that possessions are their due. They have no possessions who believe that poverty is their due. The Creator of all that is has provided enough and to spare for all. Those who provide for others are provided for. Who would not accept the good that is freely given denies the Creator who has given it. Who would not share the good they have received also denies the Creator. Accept in faith what is rightfully yours, and it will be yours. Share what you have been given, and your capacity to receive is opened wider.

TWENTY-FOUR

Joy of the flesh is a gift from the source
It is a reward, not a right
Shared with one it gives life
Shared with many it brings sorrow
True joy is in the heart, not in the flesh
The pleasure of the flesh passes, it cannot last
The joy of the heart is strong until the end
Seek the joy that lasts and be one with the source

In the world the greatest gift from the Creator is the gift of pleasure of our re-creation. If the pleasure were not greatest among all pleasures, what woman would seek the pain of birth? If the pleasure were not greatest among all pleasures, what man would leave the company of his friends? It is because of the promise of pleasure that woman and man come together. Do not take the gift from the Creator who gives all gifts, lightly. The blessing of the gift of pleasure lies in the love that bonds man to woman for the time they are in the flesh. The time of the flesh passes and cannot be recalled. The joy of love endures beyond the flesh. When man and woman can look beyond the pleasure that is of the flesh, and share the pleasure that is real, they have become one together for as long as they shall be.

TWENTY-FIVE

To be made one together is to remain one together
Woman and man are one together
Woman carries the treasure; man has been given the key
Who possesses the key does not own the treasure
Who possesses the treasure must have the key
Only when shared can the treasure be received
Treasure is not to be acquired by deceit
To deceive another is to renounce the source

Because man must be with woman to be whole, and because woman must be with man to be complete, then man and woman are one. Man does not need woman more than woman needs man. In gratitude for the gift she carries, man humbles himself before woman. In gratitude for the gift he brings, woman humbles herself before man. The pleasure that is in the gift blinds some to the wholeness that is to be gained in the sharing, and they would seek only pleasure. In seeking only their own pleasure, they deceive. One who would deceive is deceived. Deceit is a seed sown in the deceiver which yields a crop of strife. Who would deceive to gain only pleasure cannot be relied upon in anything. The greatest joy on this earth is to become one with another that life may continue to flow through your happiness. The highest achievement is to know that you are one with the Creator and complete in the trust of another That which destroys the joy, and that which conceals the power that being one with the Creator brings is the deceit of another for your own gain. The sin in pleasure is not the act itself, but betrayal of one to have pleasure with another.

TWENTY-SIX

Within the source, all are the same
The man is not greater than the woman
The parent is not greater than the child
One cannot be without the other
Man provides for woman and child
Woman provides for man and child
What the child sees is what the child learns
Show the child the source and live in peace

So that a woman might know joy, man was created. So that a man will not be lonely, woman was created. Man and woman have been created that the child may be. There is no other reason. Man, woman and child as one serve the Creator's purpose. When three are one, not one of the three is of more importance to the fulfillment of the purpose than any of the others. The seed of the Creator is planted in the Creator's fertile soil. The child produced is immortality. Man and woman will be remembered by the actions of the child. Cover yourself in glory by showing the child the true way to live. What the child is told is not the lesson the child will learn. What the child is shown is what the child will show others. Show the child respect and respect one another so that the child will respect the parents. Show the child love and love one another so that the child will love the parents. One who cannot respect and love all other cannot in turn respect and love the God who is all love. To respect and love the God who made us is the lesson we are here to learn. The lesson we are here to learn is the lesson we are to teach if we wish to live in peace.

TWENTY-SEVEN

A child is the source's perfect gift to man
The child comes in innocence
It must be taught
What man teaches the child will learn
What man has learned he will teach
Learn the world's way and live in strife
Learn the way of the Source and live in peace
What the child learns will be man's future

The gift of God to imperfect man is the perfect child. The child is the future of man, and man controls the future by what the child is taught. The child does not have a complete understanding of language, so the child must learn from what it sees. If a child sees strife, then the child learns that to cause strife is a purpose in life. If the child sees greed, then the child learns that to take from another is a purpose in life. If a child is deceived, then the child learns that deceit is the way to gain. Let those who bear children be warned that their destiny is in the hands of one they now hold. The parent who knows the way that the Creator would have us live can show the child how we must live to know the good of life. Show your child love by loving all others. Show your child peace by avoiding contention and strife. Show your child generosity by sharing with all others. When you do these things, your life will be long and old age will not be a burden.

TWENTY-EIGHT

Earth is man's gift from the source
Earth and man are one
As the earth provides for man, so man must serve the earth
What is taken must be returned
As man rests, so must the earth
Let clover grow in the corn field
Let the cattle wander
Where a rock was taken, plant a tree

When man was one of the wild things, man and the earth were one together. Earth gave man life in abundance, and man took only what was needed. Then man found wealth and demanded more. There is wealth in greater measure to take than can be taken, but care must be given to the way this wealth is gained. As man is alive, so is the earth. The earth is the air above, the sea below, the land and every living thing that grows or moves upon the land, in the sea or through the air. When too much is taken too quickly a part of the earth dies. That the earth may continue to live, treat it as you would yourself. Earth will restore itself, given time. The earth will offer up more gold, given time. But unless man can learn to respect the needs of the earth as he demands the earth meet his desires, for man there will be no more time. Will our children say, "Our parents changed Earth so that it gave up more than they needed, and in doing so they made it unable to give at all."

TWENTY-NINE

Without the mountain there would not be the valley
Without the valley there would not be the river
Without the river there would not be the sea
Without the sea there would not be the cloud
The snow that covers the mountain falls from the cloud
The sun melts the snow and the river is filled
All is one and one cannot be without the others
Be what you are, and serve as you are served

What would be served must also serve so that all will have abundance. Only man asks to receive more than he is willing to give. That is why man lives in strife. When all serve, all are served. One thing does not serve more than another. No matter how small the contribution might seem to one who gives greatly, what is small is no less vital than what is great. This is the lesson to be learned; that we are to give that which we are given so that all may have abundance and that none will have to suffer; that we are to seek those in need and serve those needs so that we may know peace; that we are to teach life to those who must be taught and lead to life those who must be lead; that we are not to look on any other as being less than we are nor look on ourselves as being greater than another. As we cannot be without others so must we be that others may be also. There is one source for all things, and we are all one in the same source. See all others as yourself, and you will know peace.

THIRTY

One who sees only the storm does not know the sea
To know the sea, one must dare the deep
The storm does not disturb the deep
The storm passes, the deep is eternal
Deep within is the source
Deep within is peace
In your time of quiet seek the peace within
Find your peace and be one with the source

Within and without are two, yet both are part of the one. The world of the spirit brings us the blessings of the flesh. Within the world of the flesh we see the workings of the spirit. Through our eyes the world of the flesh appears to be all that is, yet in the actions of others, the world of the spirit is revealed. Through our fingertips the world of the flesh is embraced, yet within our heart the world of the spirit is known. Through all our senses we see and experience the turmoil and chaos of the world of the flesh, yet within the world of turmoil and chaos is peace. To see the peace, we must look to the Spirit which is within ourselves and within all that our eyes can see. To look to the Spirit, find a place of quiet, and be still. Speak to yourself and to the Spirit that you know the Spirit is within and that you are one with it. When you are at peace with yourself, and at peace with all others-even your enemies-then the spirit will be revealed to you and all that you need will be given. It is easier to find the Spirit within when you can see beyond the turmoil and chaos of the world of the flesh to recognize the Spirit at work in all that is.

THIRTY-ONE

The source is a rock that cannot be moved
Build your house of life upon it
The source is a rain that washes away all troubles
Open your heart to its flood
The source is an ear that hears your needs
Speak to it in secret and know that you are heard
What you know will be, will be
The source can only give, so be yourself like the source

The strength of muscle and bone too quickly fades to helpless weakness. The strength that comes from the power within can only grow because its source is infinite. Nothing on this earth can prevail against the power within. When troubles seem to beset us, we find the power within to turn us away from them that they may be forgotten. When we can leave the world without and reach within to speak to the power that resides there, then that power becomes us. When we have found the power and have let it become us; when we have forgiven and forgotten all wrongs real and imagined that have been done to us; when we seek only good for all others, then whatever we can see as done is done and nothing will be denied us. When we see all that we have as a portion of unlimited abundance that is ours to claim, and give the way we expect to receive, then we will never lack for anything of be without. Whatever portion we are willing to share is the portion that is ours to claim.

THIRTY-TWO

Only the empty bowl can be filled
Only the empty heart can receive the source
Things of the world cannot fill the heart
Things of the world remain in the world
The heart that receives the source overflows
The source is eternal
One who knows the world knows death
One who knows the source knows eternal life

Each of us is a vessel into which pour the things of life. What fills our bowl is what our life will be. We choose our life by what we put in our bowl. Filled with desire for only those things that can be felt or seen our life is empty because the world of the senses is the world without. It cannot enter and fill what is within. The Source of all things, of all good, of all peace is within, yet it cannot fill us until we open ourselves to its flood. Open yourself to the flood by doing the things I have told you to do. Empty your bowl of the desire for things that only the senses can know, and let it be filled with the Soul that is eternal. To be filled with the eternal is to have all that is needed to live and rejoice in the life that is yours. One who is filled with the source lives on when the world of the senses is left behind. One who is filled with desire for the world of the senses denies the source of all that is good and eternal and will know nothing but strife and misery when the world of the senses is no more.

Chapter IX

I waited for more to be said, but my visitor was silent, I finally could not hold my curiosity in any longer, and I spoke.

"Is this all there is?" I asked.

"The Book of Wisdom is never complete. There is more:

"Are you going to tell me what it is?"

"It has not been revealed. What more is to be known will be known in its time. He stood with his hands folded in front of him and was silent. When he spoke again, it was very suddenly. "I must go," he uttered quietly.

"Not yet you aren't," I said rather firmly. I was getting a bit peeved at my visitor because he was apparently not willing to uphold his end of the bargain. "You've just walked in where you weren't in invited, somehow coerced me into taking these notes for you, and now you say you're leaving just like that. No. Not until you tell me what this is all about. Oh, yes, and the questions. You haven't answered the questions."

This outburst was very much against my nature. If I have learned one thing it is not to antagonize a man of whose nature or element you are not sure. Since my uninvited guest had not shown any reaction to my outburst, I had no notion of what its effect had been on him. I was becoming accustomed to his being here, and even felt comfortable with him. The greatest danger, however, comes from those of whom one is not wary. I quickly made the decision to become more conciliatory.

"What I meant to say is that I thought we had a bargain. I assume that I lived up to my side of it. I trust that you intend to keep yours."

"Only if you wish me to," he said quietly.

Well, of course I wished him to. After all, who doesn't want to know what God is, and even though many of us think we know the name of God's prophet it's reassuring to have our knowledge confirmed by another. The purpose of mankind is something I have pondered, and if my guest could shed light on the question, I would welcome his explanation.

"I wish so," I responded.

"Then repeat the questions, and I will answer them." "Don't you remember them?" I chided.

"What I remember is no longer important. From now on the memory must reside in you."

I had to think about that for a moment. It was quite cryptic, and I could not grasp its import-if indeed, it had any import.

"Very well," I began, "you were going to tell me what God is, who his prophet is, and what the purpose of mankind is. I am anxiously waiting to hear."

"Don't you know what God is?" he asked.

"Does anybody really know what God is?" I answered.

"You have surmised the answer," he replied.

"That is not an answer," I stammered indignantly.

"Indeed, it is," he stated emphatically. "Would you have God be infinite, all knowing, and all powerful? Then God must also be unknowable."

"That wasn't the deal," I stammered. "The bargain was that I was to take your dictation, and you were going to answer three questions for me. If you won't tell me what God is, at least tell me who God's prophet is."

"God's prophet is one who speaks the truth."

"You lied to me, didn't you? You don't know the answers any more than I do," I sputtered indignantly.

"Why do you think that?"

"You can't give me a name at is the name of the prophet?"

"I will keep my bargain," he replied with the quality in his voice that made me feel as though he were smiling at me. "In time you will realize that I have already kept my bargain, but for now I will try to give you answers you can understand." He took a deep breath, more like a prolonged sigh, and turned back to face the inky blackness of the night on the other side of the window.

Chapter X

"To know the things I will tell you, you must first know the nature of your existence. There is only one world, but it has two natures. The world you know was created from the infinite, but it is bounded by the finite. The infinite is pure and spiritual. It has no needs because from it all needs are filled. The finite creates desires and calls them needs.

"What is finite is temporary. What is spiritual is eternal. I have just given you the Book of Wisdom. It tells you all this, but I will tell you these things again.

"What is real is unseen. It can be compared to the wind. Who has seen the wind? When a tree bends, we say the wind bends it, yet the force that bends it is invisible to us. When a force pushes against our face and makes it cold, we say it is the wind, yet nothing is seen. When screams are heard from trees or from the rigging of a ship, we say it is the wind, yet we look, and nothing is there. So, it is with The Infinite. Our view of it is limited by the tools of the finite; our eyes, our fingertips, our ears, our tongue, and our nose. Like the wind, only evidence of the infinite can be found. The Infinite itself is unseen and unknown.

"What evidence do we have of The Infinite? The tassel of corn that becomes the grain that feeds us, the rain from the sky that springs from the rock and quenches our thirst, the tiny nut that become the tree that gives us shade or walls for our house.

"The Infinite comes to us as our other half whose life, combined with our own, makes us whole and frees us from loneliness. In wholeness we share with it in creation, and The Infinite reveals its presence in the new life it brings from our loins. ?"

"The Infinite is seen in the stranger who is kind. It is in our hands when we comfort one in pain, in our words when we bring hope to one in despair, in our lips when we smile and let our joy touch another. When our feet rush to the victim in need, The Infinite has shown them the way. The Infinite is revealed to us also by the words of the prophets who have found its presence.

"Who is the true prophet? If the Infinite is unknowable can we the finite have the wisdom to say who speaks its truth? To know who speaks truth, first know what truth is. Truth is that which cannot be debated. Truth remains constant no matter how many times it is tested. Who speaks the truth is the true prophet."

"Does the true prophet have a name," I asked very tentatively. " Yes," he replied without explanation.

"Then what is it?" I asked more boldly. "One Who Speaks The Truth."

I almost became exasperated by his evasiveness, but just as I was about to blurt out an expletive preparatory to accusing him of not knowing what he was talking about a feeling of calm came over me. I felt the smile from the shadow of the cowl. He continued before I could speak.

"You see, men have accepted the words of men as truth. The have given the speaker power over their lives in his name only. In the name they have built temples. In the name they have killed those who claim another name for their prophet. In the name they have forsaken truth. They bow before the idol that is the name, and the words of truth that were spoken by the one who has the name are forgotten. Truth makes all men one. It does not divide."

"I see," I told him.

"If you do, then you can answer the last question," he said quietly. "Yes, I can," I replied in the same tone of voice.

"Then my purpose here has been filled. You are entrusted with the Book of Wisdom. Guard it well and live its truths," and with those words he ceased to be.

I rubbed my eyes in disbelief. Someone had been standing by my window, and now-very suddenly-no one was standing by my window. I looked all around the small room. I was its only occupant. There were only four walls, the cot, the table and two chairs, and the pegs on the wall from which my clothes and my sea bag hung.

I arose from my chair and rushed to the door. Dawn was breaking, but in the dim light only the village could be seen. A rooster greeted the emerging morning just as I stepped out into it, but no other sign of life was evident. Who was my visitor, and where had he gone?

"It must have been a dream," I told myself as I turned and reentered the hut. But there on the table lay this sheaf of strange paper and the pages I had filled out in the night. Had it not been for this paper I would indeed have believed it a hallucination, but it is too unique to be denied.

Another thing struck me as strange. When he had appeared to me, it had been early in the night. Now, here it was dawn and I was not the least bit sleepy. As a matter of fact, I felt quite rested.

I have been reading and contemplating the words I wrote down that strange night for almost a week now, and they are committed to memory. This morning, the Indian who has been my guide to the ruins came to me to tell me of an expedition which as arrived at a ruin about two days travel from here. In addition to conversation with others who speak my language, I hope to find someone there who will take this package from me and put it aboard a ship bound for home.

I myself have one more great quest before leaving here for other places. I have heard tales of a tribe that lives in a hidden valley somewhere north of here. It is said that while the tribe is known, their land is not. No one has seen their villages. How exciting it will be to be the first to discover their whereabouts.

My great uncle Ezra's writing ended there. My curiosity was piqued. I wanted to know more about the man who was a link in my chain of ancestry, but apparently, I already knew all that there was to know. I looked back into the envelope in the hope that there was something else in there. I didn't see anything else, but I turned it upside down and shook it anyway. A slip of paper with the same writing on it fell out. The handwriting was Ezra's. At the time I read it, it didn't make much sense.

The corn we eat tomorrow grows from the seed we plant today
 A stronger foe can be defeated by a better plan
Plant the seed, not the crop
Plan the battle, not the victory

What an inheritance this was. The only thing I could think about was what Heidi was going to say when she realized that I had spent our cash and increased our debt for a bunch of old letters. I stuck it all in a bag I had brought for the purpose of bringing back loot and left the attic. I took my flight back Houston on Sunday, well fed and rested.

On a whim I had taken the little silver spoon and the china doll into a local antique dealer to find out if they had any value at all. To my delight, they were deemed ancient enough to be considered rare, and the price I got for them paid for meals and a modest hotel room.

Epilogue

It turned out that there was immense treasure in the bag I brought back with me, and it made our family fabulously wealthy. It wasn't the gold mine stock, though. Research into that revealed that Great Columbia Gold Mine was a scam from the beginning. The wealth was in the Book of Wisdom that Ezra had sent from the jungles of Guatemala.

The wealth we have also isn't the kind that can be counted. It's hard to explain to someone who has to see luxury to believe in wealth, but wealth is really lack of fear about tomorrow. What I've come to realize about it is that what we call wealth is one of the greatest curses we can carry around with us. With wealth there is never enough, and if someone has more then we have to have less. To get more we have to risk what we have, and in risk there is fear.

Through the Book of Wisdom, I have also found peace. It is difficult to continue to live our lives in turmoil when we stop focusing on our own unfulfilled desires, and instead look for ways to fulfill the needs of others. Doing this sure brought peace to our marriage.

It didn't happen overnight, but it looks like Heidi and I are going to be a couple forever. Not only that, but we are going to be a couple forever that likes each other as friends as well as enjoying each other as lovers.

What started it was me forgetting all the things about her that annoyed me and working on finding out what the things were about me that really annoyed her. The first step we took together was to pick a time that was just ours. Our time meant just that. No kids, no TV, no other distractions, and we just talked. Of course, the first tthing I felt I needed to do was explain that I wanted to try to correct some of the mistakes I had made in the past which gave her an opportunity to unload on me about what an in-considerate bastard I had been. I felt that she spent an inordinate amount of time on that subject. The next thing that happened was that I lost the job that I hated and started doing something I really liked. After I started learning how to be honest about things, I decided to be honest about how I felt in regard to the boring work I was doing. In most cases it probably isn't wise to be as candid with a boss as I was with mine, but-what the heck-I was new at this honesty thing at the time so I could be expected to make a few mistakes.

Anyhow, I felt compelled to tell him that I wasn't happy doing what I was doing which compelled him to tell me that for a long time he hadn't been happy with what I was doing either. This led to a conversation about what would I be happy doing, and the only thing I could think of was to fix up the yard. He commented on what a good job I had done on it so far and asked if I would consider landscaping a new place they had just moved into. What came out of the whole incident involving my resignation-which at one point had been precariously close to being my firing-was that I got my first job as a landscape contractor as well as a fairly generous severance package. After his landscaping was in, the now ex-boss bankrolled Heidi and me in our own garden supply and nursery business.

Watching us get along together worked wonders with the kids. Not only that, but they quit lying to us. Of course, we had to quit lying to them first. Lying did not encompass Santa Claus or the Easter Bunny for the youngest, but it also did not mean inventing fabulous tales to perpetuate the myths. We found out that, "I don't know." as an answer did not result in any loss of respect from them, either. Of course, "I don't know," resulted in all of us working together to find the answer, if the asker and the askee both thought the question was deserving enough to put forth the effort. Sometimes the answer was "I can't tell you that right now," if it was something, we had promised someone else not to tell.

If one thing has to be named as the most important lesson that our family got from the Book it has to be honesty. One comment about what I mean by honesty is how it should be handled to take care that it doesn't hurt another. It's like warts. Telling somebody they have warts is unnecessary and may even be wrong.

That pretty much covers my comments on the Book, and what it has meant to us. Its truth has been handed down in many forms by many others. This is just one more volume in the library of lore that attempts to get the message out to those who are looking for it but haven't yet found the medium through which they can receive it. All I can say in closing is that it works.

www.ingramcontent.com/pod-product-compliance
Lightning Source LLC
LaVergne TN
LVHW020433080526
838202LV00055B/5170